Hues of Sundown

Sadie Hussain

BookLeaf Publishing

Presentation by *BookLeaf Publishing*

Web: www.bookleafpub.com

E-mail: info@bookleafpub.com

ISBN: 9789357212236

First edition 2023

Still

If only for a moment we close our eyes,
To discover the melodies of the Universe,

If only we can close our ears,
To gaze at Mother Earth in her natural splendor,

If only we can be silent,
We shall behold the beauty of a still Soul,

Be Silent, surrender and be still my Soul.

Epiphany

It is only in suspension, mid-flight, no landing in sight, that we subject our wings to the unfolding, an epiphany, beginning the unfamiliar voyage.

And as we fly, we still may not comprehend the trajectory or course, but the miracle lies in the expansion, the spreading of wings.

You may not know where you are going or where it will all end, but just know that so long as you spread your wings, the winds will somehow carry you.

Dragon

Known to swim against currents, battling great obstacles through perseverance,

Strength, courage and patience; everything that embodies koi no takinobori,

Perhaps the ancient metaphor and mysticism is what overwhelms me with beauty or perhaps it is the praise for adversity that draws me to the Koi's splendor.

The most beautiful people I have known and loved are those who have known defeat, known suffering, known hardship and have found their way out of the depths.

Beautiful people do not just exist, they evolve.

The harshest conditions often lead to the greatest moments in life and it is adversity that births the resilience and courage, so that one can flourish into the Dragon.

Torn

I'm torn,

Between the mountains and the oceans, my spirit is torn,

Beyond the Earth, beyond the furthest skies, I'm torn.

Fire

Abysmal heart;

Infinite, beyond horizons;

Deeper than oceans;

Didn't you know? It is the light of your love that
sets the sky ablaze.

Dark

Could it be that light does not travel faster than anything after all,

For, no matter how fast its voyage, it's discovery,

Darkness had always got there first, submissive, waiting to be devoured,

Drenched in light.

You

When I say "You", I mean a thousand universes,

Vast mysteries of the dark, undiscovered.

Woman

"Lover" says he, the one that comforts my
insecurities, the one that heals my Soul,

"Mama" says he, the one that sleeps in my
embrace, my precious heart,

"Daughter" says her, the one that sees through
me, her bosom is my abode,

And "Sister" they say, the keepers, the tribe.

True

There is a strength in your surrender,

In your submission, in your acquiescence,

There lies victory in your softness, the courage
in opening your heart, displaying vulnerability,
innocence,

There lies all of you, in all your raw humanity,
your primitive essence,

True form.

Hard

It is hard not to look at the world through a lens of pain,

To scorn at the rose, in your loathing of the thorn,

To sum up your blessings in a world so cruel, so cold.

Death Wish

How many times do we wish days may pass,
forgetting, that it is our life,

Our longing to accelerate time, a fickle desire,
a failure to be present.

Submission

I kissed the Earth in my submission,

Like leaves on a tree, seduced to the ground,

And then I silently wished;

"Peace be upon my Soul".

Antidote

I yearned to release all my hearts' sorrows when you arrive,

But how can I fulfill the promise to myself?

All sadness dispels at the moment you grace me.

Melody

Refine your hearts' ability to tune in and
recognize what serves your purpose,

Erode at your ego,

Be still,

Meditate,

Align within and witness the unfolding,

A delicate opening of perspective,

Listen deeply and you will hear just how
profound is the melody of your Soul.

Confidence

Confidence is the art of owning ones' survival,

A primitive display of resilience.

So when you falter in your steps, repeat:

"Survive".

Micro-Insights

A sigh,

Tears,

The hesitancy in a smile,

A soft touch,

A frown,

Not all that is felt can be articulated.

And so; emerged the nuances of expression,

Micro-insights of "Self".

Godly

I look at him and see God.

Not in the sense that I see our Creator,

But proof that he is His Creation.

Phoenix

Sometimes, the Eagle inside of me alights in retreat, bewildered.

The Wolf caged inside my ribs shrinks into the shadows, fragmented.

There are nights when the Lioness cedes in her enervation, she cannot live to fight another day.

But then there lies in my soul, the Phoenix, who embraces me in her wings and whispers gallantly:

"Rise from the ashes, You Will Rise".

Bibliophile

When I ask you to open my cover and read
through the poems of my Soul,

I do not mean that you run your fingers along
the lexes and glean on my annotations,

I bid you to savor the words on your lips, to lick
the innuendos and relish the flavors on your
tongue so to taste me.

Freedom

If freedom was a person, she would be a voyager,

Uninhibited, liberated,

She would be unapologetic, merciful, defiant in her wit,

Carnal in her charm and loathed for her grit.

Pariah

We cull the dark in foolhardiness,

Little comprehension of its worth,

After all, how can one marvel at the breaking of
Dawn,

Without grasping the depth of the Night.

www.ingramcontent.com/pod-product-compliance
Lightning Source LLC
Chambersburg PA
CBHW062112140826
49812CB00058B/1309
* 9 7 8 9 3 5 7 2 1 2 2 3 6 *